## PRAISE FOR HERA LINDSAY BIRD

"Recently ran across a New Zealand poet, Hera Lindsay Bird, who does a version of what I used to do, but does it 100x better." —David Berman

"Frank and outrageous . . . it has made me, like many others, more excited about poetry than I have been in a long time." —*Guardian*

"Full of outrageous guilty pleasures. She writes with the cheek of Frank O'Hara." —*Telegraph*

"Funny, clever and deadpan and kept me hanging on every line. . . . Her writing has a freshness and straightforwardness that strides confidently off the page." —Jon McGregor, *Observer*

"The deadpan comic bravado of the New Zealand poet Hera Lindsay Bird looks literary decorum in the eye and dares it to blush."

—Jeremy Noel-Tod, *Sunday Times*

"A literary phenomenon . . . goofy, funny and tender, her energy and sensitivity will captivate." —*Elle*

"Without doubt the most arresting and original new young poet, on the page and in performance." —Carol Ann Duffy

"If you have forgotten what a poem is, you should read Hera Lindsay Bird's poems. if you haven't forgotten what a poem is, you should forget immediately and then read Hera Lindsay Bird's poems."

—Kimmy Walters

# Juvenilia

OTHER BOOKS AVAILABLE BY HERA LINDSAY BIRD

*Hera Lindsay Bird*

*Pamper Me to Hell & Back*

# *Juvenilia*

## Hera Lindsay Bird

Illustrated by Gino Dal Cin

DEEP VELLUM PUBLISHING
DALLAS, TEXAS

Deep Vellum Publishing
3000 Commerce St., Dallas,Texas 75226
deepvellum.org · @deepvellum

Deep Vellum is a 501c3 nonprofit literary arts organization
founded in 2013 with the mission to bring
the world into conversation through literature.



Support for this publication has been provided in part by grants from the National Endowment for the Arts, the Texas Commission on the Arts, the City of Dallas Office of Arts and Culture, the Communities Foundation of Texas, and the Addy Foundation.

ISBNs: 978-1-64605-377-3 (paperback) | 978-1-64605-390-2 (ebook)

LIBRARY OF CONGRESS CATALOGING-IN-PUBLICATION DATA
Names: Bird, Hera Lindsay, author.
Title: Juvenilia / Hera Lindsay Bird.
Description: Dallas, Texas : Deep Vellum Publishing, 2025.
Identifiers: LCCN 2024055489 (print) | LCCN 2024055490 (ebook) | ISBN 9781646053773 (trade paperback) | ISBN 9781646053902 (ebook)
Subjects: LCGFT: Poetry.
Classification: LCC PR9639.4.B55 J88 2025 (print) | LCC PR9639.4.B55 (ebook) | DDC 821/.92--dc23/eng/20241120
LC record available at https://lccn.loc.gov/2024055489
LC ebook record available at https://lccn.loc.gov/2024055490

Front cover design by Gino Dal Cin
Interior Layout and Typesetting by KGT

PRINTED IN CANADA

CONTENTS

## WRITE A BOOK

To be fourteen, and wet yourself extravagantly
At a supermarket checkout
As urine cascades down your black lace stocking
And onto the linoleum
Is to comprehend what it means to be a poet
To stand in the tepid under-halo
Of your own self-making
And want to die . . .
Far away, in a field of wild orchids
Is a backwards sentimentality
Like a Christmas card with the robins scratched out
Well, it was Oscar Wilde who said sentimentality
is *the desire to have the luxury of an emotion without paying for it*
Like . . . when I masturbate and think of nuns
but never go to church at Christmas
Now I have a Masters degree in poetry and no longer wet myself
But I still have to die in antiquated flowers
Does this make me sentimental?
Well, who's to judge?
You can get away with anything in a poem
As long as you say my tits in it
But it's a false courage to be so modestly endowed
And have nothing meaningful to say
You might think this book is ironic
But to me, it is deeply sentimental
like . . . if you slit your wrists while winking—does that make it a joke?
To be alive
Is the greatest sentimentality there is
And I live to be sentimental
And I love to be alive

Always weeping at the end of a movie
Over the frosted carriages of yesteryear
I wrote this book, and it is sentimental
Because I don't have a right-sized reaction to the world
To write a book is not a right-sized reaction
To put all your bad thoughts on paper
And make someone else pay for them
My friend says it's bad poetry to write a book
And I agree with her
I agree with her . . . in principle
But I wrote a book anyway
And I named it after myself
My name is Hera Lindsay Bird
This book is called Hera Lindsay Bird
I wrote it, and I mean at least 75% of it
And if that's not sentimental
Well . . .
One day I'm going to have to pay for it

# SUMMER

## IF YOU ARE AN ANCIENT EGYPTIAN PHARAOH

I am carving dirty hieroglyphics
into the wall of your tomb
If you are a dead French aristocrat
I am the suspicious circumstances
surrounding your death
If you are a shape-shifting wizard
I am the shape you are shifting into
If you are a fast-moving cloud
I am an entire field of deer
looking up
If you are a sceptical cop
I am a haunted fax machine
If you are a catapult
I am the medieval knight
you are catapulting
I fly over the dark fields of my enemies
corkscrewing the dawn
This is what missing you feels like
Without you
I am just the suspicious circumstances
surrounding nothing
Without you I am just
a regular medieval knight
settling ongoing tenancy disputes
and doing other knight-related activities
like dying thousands of years ago
I rise from the grave to lean
like an ancient wind against your house
Your roof a red eyelid
closed against the sky

When I'm not with you I am like
a lonely wrestler with nobody to break chairs on
When you take off your clothes
the whole room darkens to light you
Your nakedness a pale kite
In the centre of the room

I want to take you to the river that runs behind my house
and show you where the dark water vanishes between the rocks
but I can't
because nothing runs behind my house
not even a lonely commercial highway
I want to stand with you
on the edge of a lonely commercial highway
waiting for the jumper cables
that will restart this engine
and take us somewhere far beyond
the confines of this poem

I need to have a reason
for the aisles of trees we sailed through
and your hand on my knee in reckless disregard
of road safety recommendations
I need to have a reason
for so many nights of watching you recede from me
like the ass end of a horse
in the credits of a Western
I need to have a reason
for drinking beer in your parents' swimming pool at night
and how you lay face down in the water
like a body in a celestial crime scene
The stars so many knives
in the small of your back

# CHILDREN ARE THE ORGASM OF THE WORLD

This morning on the bus there was a woman carrying a bag with inspirational sayings and positive affirmations which I was reading because I'm a fan of inspirational sayings and positive affirmations. I also like clothing that gives you advice. What's better than the glittered baseball cap of a stranger telling you what to strive for? It's like living in a world of endless therapists. The inspirational bag of the woman on the bus said a number of things like 'live in the moment' and 'remember to breathe' but it also said 'children are the orgasm of the world'. Are children the orgasm of the world like orgasms are the orgasms of sex? Are children the orgasm of anything? Children are the orgasm of the world like hovercraft are the orgasm of the future or silence is the orgasm of the telephone, or shit is the orgasm of the lasagne. You could even say sheep are the orgasm of lonely pastures, which are the orgasm of modern farming practices which are the orgasm of the industrial revolution. And then I thought why not? I like comparing things to other things too. Like sometimes when we're having sex and you look like a helicopter in a low-budget movie, disappearing behind a cloud to explode. Or an athlete winning a prestigious sporting tournament at the exact moment he realises his wife has been kidnapped. For the most part, orgasms are the orgasms of the world. Like slam-dunking a glass basketball. Or executing a perfect dive into a swimming pool full of oh my god. Or travelling into the past to forgive yourself and creating a time paradox so complex it forces all of human history to reboot, stranding you naked on some rocky outcrop, looking up at the sunset from a world so new looking up hasn't even been invented yet.

# I WANT TO GET HIGH MY WHOLE LIFE WITH YOU

I feel it in my leather hotpant pockets
I feel it in my anime wind blowing through an alpine tennis resort
overcome with wildflowers
I feel it in my ironic valley girl hairflip
I feel it in my admittedly limited knowledge of the Roman mythologies
I feel it in my biopic about a corrupt alcoholic educational resource
salesman advertising increasingly less and less educational resources

I want to get high my whole life with you
i feel it in my anime wind blowing through an alpine tennis resort
overcome with wildflowers AGAIN and the poem isn't even halfway over
yet
so what if my blood is the wind
so what if I love you so much I am becoming stupid
my heart melting like red candles on Satan's birthday cake

I want to get high with you out the back of a family funeral
I want to get high with you at an industrial carpet outlet store
I want to get high with you at the top of the Grand Canyon and scream
and pretend like you're going to push me in even though I know you
pushing me in is the last thing you want because if you did that I'd die
and you don't want me to die
I love you so much I tell you about it
I love you so much I have already picked out my grave
and written your name on it
when you laugh in the dark
it fills the room with a thousand upside-down cartoon bats

how dare you be the kind of person I would immediately fall completely
in love with
and be devastated if you left
how dare you come and do that
your eyes
like two black cats
licking their assholes
in the hot morning sun of my face

O this feeling has turned my skeleton pink
with you I feel my mind changing
with you I feel my blood changing
I want to get really good at woodwork
I want to get really good at woodwork
and go into the forest
and cut up some logs
and make you a beautiful house to live in

# THE DA VINCI CODE

It was a hot summer morning, five hundred years ago in Italy, and Leonardo da Vinci was busy at work inventing the modern helicopter.

He stood in his workshop with the sun beating down on his various ancient-looking parchments and took a sip from a historically accurate beverage out of a historically accurate cup. Suddenly, a long-dead bird came flying into his workshop half a century ago! Leonardo da Vinci laughed anciently, like a great man from the past might. He went out onto his balcony and looked out over all the brick-coloured houses made by dead Italian people, stacked to the tits with frescoes and ivies and little brown dogs running everywhere and people carrying loaves of bread around in their arms, like soft gluten purses, like vigilante mayors of breadtown. "I love ancient Italy! It's my home," he thought while simultaneously inventing a complicated water device with lots of intricate levers and screws thats too hard to explain to normal-level intelligence people but rest assured it was good.

He leapt hugely off his balcony and went for a tall walk down the street, becoming constantly inspired by observing the world and all the momentous inventions he was going to invent for it. If electricity had been invented he might have waited for a traffic light, but he didn't have time to invent electricity today, or traffic either, or even to play the lyre beautifully with his long homosexual fingers. He was late for the first day of the Italian Renaissance!!!

When he got to the first day of the Italian Renaissance, Michelangelo and Botticelli and Italian Shakespeare were there plus a lot of other famous dead guys listed on the Wikipedia page and they had all taken the day off from their jobs which was painting giant winged babies for art and doing heaps of other famous and enlightened things like making up classical philosophies and growing massive beards out of chin modesty.

"I have invented the helicopter!!!!!" Leonardo da Vinci shouted, striding into the official Renaissance headquarters, knocking several large tables over and absentmindedly punching a grandfather clock in its big ticking face before stopping time for a few minutes, and then inventing time again but even more accurate than the first time around. "Damn, I love being an inventor," he said, and kissed several handsome young nearby men who all loved it, mouth-wise.

"What is a helicopter?" Michelangelo asked, like a little bitch. Michelangelo was jealous because the only thing he ever invented was painting on ceilings which is a dumb place to put art because you have to lie down to look at it and get the back of your head all dirty.

But Leonardo laughed because that was the kind of guy he WAS, the kind of guy who knew what helicopters were before they even existed, before even the kinds of metals that could make them fly were dug out of the earth, only he wasn't laughing in a mean way, but in a joyful and ahead of his time kind of way.

A helicopter is a machine for flying, he explained and showed them his drawings which were museum quality and rare looking. Then Botticelli was like, "Well what does a helicopter do?" and Leonardo recounted the entire plot of Mission Impossible which he also invented on the spot and did all the noises for including the part where Tom Cruise is climbing along the top of a moving train with his skin getting wrinkled because the train is going so fast and then he sees a train tunnel coming up and ties the helicopter to the train and the helicopter has to fly through the tunnel and Tom Cruise nearly gets decapitated by the helicopter blade but doesn't and divorces Katie Holmes and the train driver looks up through the window at him as if to say, "Did you really just tie a helicopter to my train inside a train tunnel and blow it up? That's really dangerous. Katie Holmes is too good for you," and then Tom Cruise takes off his sunglasses and says, "Mission impossible, more like mission . . . accomplished," and everyone from the Italian Renaissance just bursts into tears because they've never heard of Tom Cruise before, nobody had, da Vinci invented him too, as a private joke.

"You're really good at this Renaissance thing," Italian Shakespeare said to him, stunned and overwhelmed, but da Vinci was so humble he was just like, "Thanks, your friendship means a lot to me," and then suggested they all move on to lay the foundations for capitalism and banking.

At the end of the first day of the Italian Renaissance, Leonardo da Vinci walked home through the picturesque streets of his historical birthplace and at the fading sunlight which looked like an enormous fire burning somewhere very far away, which of course he knew astronomically it was, and at all the black cats yawing hugely with their long-dead mouths and the flowers on the windowsills completely fucking abundant with bees and thought with a happy tear in his eye, "I wish I was still alive," because of course he knew himself to be already dead in the future, he was that brilliant. His genius was both a blessing and a curse. He couldn't see flowers without inventing a vase to put them in. He couldn't stare directly into the sun without inventing a pair of tinted aviators. He couldn't see a beautiful man without inventing a kiss directly onto his mouth

Leonardo spent the rest of his life inventing cool things and drawing famous paintings and even a picture of a guy with four arms and four legs rolling around inside a huge circle for medical students to put on their pencil cases in the future. He looked up at the sky and knew scientifically why it was blue, but that didn't stop him from thinking it was beautiful and in later years when he died and went to heaven God was like, "Don't tell the others but you're my favourite of all my children," which made Jesus super mad, but Jesus didn't invent anything except for eternal life and who wants that, Da Vinci didn't, he wanted to be a big pile of homosexual forever bones so he said, "Thanks but no thanks," stole a mousepad from heaven's giftshop and came back to us here on earth, where we still visit his bones to this day and say, These Were The Bones Of A Great Man, he wore them inside his body like a meat clotheshanger, he wore them like a wild horse wears the skeleton of the wind, he wore them towards the possibility of the future which he was inventing as he rode the horse of his own mind onward, whispering the name of beautiful things to come and in doing so, calling them forward into existence, he wore them like patience and was kind to all who knew him. Goodbye Leonardo DV you extraordinary son of a bitch goodbye goodbye we love and miss you every day.

# I AM SO IN LOVE WITH YOU I WANT TO LIE DOWN IN THE MIDDLE OF A MAJOR PUBLIC INTERSECTION AND CRY

is not how you're supposed to start love poems
but I'm too far gone
to work up to it gently

your naked back in the mirror
has cured at least three to four major diseases

for you, I would set myself on fire in a smoke detector factory
for you, I would ride through the mall on a Segway knocking juices out of the hands
of thirsty real estate agents

your lungs like Christmas stockings waiting for Santa to climb down the chimney and put cancer in
your face like the face of a dead French revolutionary
in an out-of-date children's textbook
my stupid heart . . . like a snow globe . . . filled with blood

If you left me, I would be forced to gaze despairingly into the middle distance
If you left me I would be forced to emotionally distance myself from the situation as a self-preservation technique until eventually I healed enough to be able to consider romantic relationships with other people, all the time secretly resenting you for failing to sustain your attraction to me despite the totally involuntary & uncontrollable nature of human desire

your teeth like a graveyard ........ in springtime
your tongue like a mattress ........ in a graveyard ............ in springtime

your tongue on my cunt like a mattress ........ in a graveyard ............ in springtime

my pubic hair like the black carpet on the Titanic
my ass ............................ like an ass buffet

you put me in a friendly but uncompromising headlock
you bite me all over my neck and shoulders!!!!!

i don't know how to write a love poem
because love is indescribable
it's this feeling you get
when your mind gets hot
and everything else gets insignificant .................... with diamonds on it
and you have to laugh and laugh at things in your second-hand dress

the slow rising of your eyelid
like a girl's skirt
my eyes like two envelopes stuffed with snow
and no return address
my eyes like pair of pale blue cowboy boots
walking slowly down the street towards you

it's like
you've finally found someone that interests you
and you get more and more interested
like a fascinating disease

it's like
for some reason, you have to think of the Wild West all the time
but it doesn't make any sense???
because you don't really care about the Wild West!!!

it's better than tv

to look at someone and feel so much happiness
your smile a single arrow, quivering in a tree trunk

it's like . . . life is not a punishment
and sometimes good things happen for no reason

I stare and stare at you like a distant mountain in a homoeopathic video game
with rare & medicinal flowers on it

# WAYS OF MAKING LOVE

*After Bernadette Mayer*

Like a metal detector detecting another metal detector.
Like two lonely scholars in the dark clefts of the Cyrillic alphabet.

Like an ancient star slowly getting sucked into a black hole.
So hard we break televised sport, leaving the conveners of the Olympics
with a generous redundancy package.

You're a denim tree and I'm the world's fastest autumn.
I am the entire Roman Republic, and you are Hannibal
taking me from behind.
You stride into council chambers, waving a petition to orgasm.

A lip of cloud brushes the roof of the barn.
The pale trees curve around the eye and back into the brain.

It's like watching porn through a kaleidoscope
or a slow wind in a kite factory.
Like dogs trying to do it people-style but failing
due to the inflexibility of their anatomical structures.

A cloud of bats floats slowly up into your brain rafters.
You roll down my stockings, like the sun peeling ocean from a Soviet globe.

I want you in a seventeenth-century field, tilling the earth like flesh tractors.
In the red shade of a mammoth
in the Natural History Museum.
In the airlock of a space station, my heart shaking
like an epileptic star.
Between the plastic sheets of a lobotomy table

because writing poetry about fucking
when you could be fucking
is the last refuge of the stupid.

It's like getting three wishes and wishing for less wishes.
It's like designing a flag the exact same colour as the sky.
It's like crying over spilled milk before it's out of the cow.
It's like breaking into a field at dawn
and euthanising the cow so you can get your crying over and done with
and immediately begin adjusting to your new lactose-free existence.
But love isn't really like killing cattle
no matter what poetry wants us to believe.

The day is a vault the sun has cracked
money flying everywhere like really expensive leaves
and here I am begging you to come back
as if you were already gone

## LOST SCROLLS

*After Mark Leidner*

Like a passive-aggressive gun that fires . . . nothing instead of bullets
Or Nostradamus predicting the invention of the Capri pant . . .
Like a primaeval tornado collecting nothing but air . . .

Like accidentally wishing on a satellite and getting women's golf instead
of happiness . . .
Like your dad threatening to turn the planet around and keep driving . . .
Like throwing your wedding bouquet backwards into a discount sporting
goods store . . .

Like substituting inspirational quotes for inspirational estimates
or dawn through a magnifying glass
Like slowly fingering your girlfriend to Bohemian Rhapsody . . .

It should be like being buried in a denim-lined coffin . . .
But it's dollhouse curtains flapping in the breeze

It should be a bouquet of lilacs shackled to your ankle . . .
But it's black milk pouring out of the fountain . . .

It's like freezing containers of vomit to reheat and pour down the toilet . . .
Or the mice in your teenage son's walls, listening to Einstürzende
Neubauten
It's like an advent calendar for atheists full of empty windows

It's like squeezing your mop into a tropical fish tank
Or drinking Gatorade in your wedding dress
It's like a garden salad thrown into the blades of a helicopter

It's like something that cannot be said but must be said . . . and in being said
slows the rapid expansion...of the prison-industrial complex . . .
It's like your family commissioning a shrugging angel headstone . . .

It should be like tits at dawn . . .
or a million trees in winter . . .
But it's like setting the planet on fire . . . by letting your kite fly too close to the sun

It's like saving millions on camouflage gear by getting Russia a to invest in smart-casual trees . . .

It's like being so committed to living each day as if it were your last, you spend each afternoon having a cerebral haemorrhage in a rest home . . .

Your neighbourhood is involved in a gang war and you are trying to stay neutral by wearing white, and your neighbour is stabbing you repeatedly in the chest whispering *White is not a colour, it's a shade . . .*

It's summer on the Rio Grande and ten thousand bees fly towards you in the shape of your father and say . . . *What do you mean you're quitting baseball? . . .*

It's like falling in love for the first time for the last time . . .
Or your dead wife returning to you in the body of a convicted paedophile . . .
It's like when you're a ghost, and you can feel the wind blow in through
your sheetholes

It's like a tornado in a harmonica shop,
or a suicide note burned into a cornfield . . .
It's like using a mnemonic device based on complex chemical structures to
remember your mother's name . . .

It should be like a film adaptation of the Home Alone novelisations . . .
But it's like writing the word hunger in gravy . . .

It should be like fucking in a casket . . .
But it's sunlight falling on castle stones . . .

It's like punching someone in the face and saying *just kidding* . . .
Or trying to find your way out a door museum . . .
It's the black wind through the maples, and the difficulty of getting tenure . . .

It's like loading a catapult with a catapult and catapulting it into irony . . .
Or a baby singing itself to sleep . . .
It's like a post-apocalyptic petting zoo, with cages full of old fur coats . . .

It's like panicking because your castle is too beautiful
Or pushing a pram through the dawn
But the pram is on fire, because the fire is your baby
It's like having an orgasm every time you hear middle C on a piano
Mozart is just foreplay to you

It's like the bonus level on Tekken where you punch a man's face so hard
he becomes the evil version of himself . . .
But there's no such thing . . . as punching a man's face so hard
he becomes the evil version of himself . . .
There's no such thing as the evil version of anything . . .
It's like a movie where everything started out fine
and continued to be fine
until at the end of the movie it turned out everything had been fine all along

That's what love is like . . .
It's like firing a gun into a time machine and accidentally hitting Hitler . . .
It's like masturbating to a documentary on South African mines and
ejaculating real diamonds . . .
It's like wanting something so bad you would die to have it . . .
But you do have it and nobody is asking you to die . . .

Not the civil war re-enactors loading their muskets in the field behind the
supermarket parking lot . . .
Not the man on the bus, with the Ted Bundy biography
Not even the entire American military complex . . .

Every night you come over and we watch some film . . .
about people sprinting through the corridors of an abandoned space
station . . .
or
being stabbed to death . . . in the glittering wetlands of Louisiana . . .
and every night nobody comes to our house . . .
and murders us in our sleep . . .

# AUTUMN

# UPON WAKING IN A MOTEL ROOM I BECOME IMMEDIATELY CONVINCED THAT YOU NO LONGER LOVE ME AND BURST INTO TEARS

Not only that, but maybe you never loved me in the first place

I lean against the window like a woman in a film
with the word buffalo in the title
It's easy for me to make myself sad by thinking of you as a dead soldier
You, and all my other civil war boyfriends
who died so young & well-endowed
their fresh hearts riding the grass
They died so long ago I forget they were real
I bet some of them were real
I bet some of them stood upon the brink of their lives in great
astonishment
I can't be the only one
I can't be the only one to feel so weird all the time

I don't know what I dreamed that made me call you
You sounded tired and hung up to buy cigarettes

I know you love me
because I can feel it when you look at me
your eyes like evil black suns
burning all my kites off
I turned on the TV & started watching *Indian in the Cupboard*
and then turned it off again
I lay down, thinking of small campfires in the dark

I don't know what to do about my love for you
it goes on and on like history

I change my screensaver to a white horse on an overcast day
standing knee deep in a field of flowers
Sometimes a picture can feel as real as the thing itself
Sometimes a poem can feel as real as the thing itself

I think if I had to choose between you and poetry I'd choose poetry,
but I'd always think about you
I'd always think about you
and wonder what you were doing

# THE EX-GIRLFRIENDS ARE BACK FROM THE WILDERNESS

The ex-girlfriends are back . . .
emerging once again from the tree shadows . . .
into the primordial burlesque of autumn
with their low-cut . . .
reminiscences . . . and soft, double ironies . . .
trembling once again into their
opulent . . .
seasonal migration patterns
a corsage of wilting apologies
tethered to the bust . . .

The ex-girlfriends are back . . .with their
hand-beaded inconsistencies . . .
& various unhappy motives . . .
dragging their heart like a soft broom through leaves . . .
and they go on hurting . . . like the lit windows
of a dollhouse in winter . . .
with a too-big horse outside . . .

The ex-girlfriends are back
but in a romantically ambiguous way . . .

The ex-girlfriends are back and have transcended
the patriarchal limitations of romance . . .
unlike the new girlfriends . . .
still handcuffed to monogamy . . .
slowly writhing . . .
with their naughty . . . post-heterosexual fatalism

The ex-girlfriends are back
with their unfounded Soviet aspirations . . .
and anti-hegemonic arts initiatives . . .
draped over a piano on the edge of the thicket
playing the lonely upper hand of chopsticks . . .
in their vague tropical displeasure . . .

The ex-girlfriends are back . . .
and the post-girlfriends . . .
and the 'let's not put a label on this' girlfriends . . .
all of them at the same time, walking out through
a beaded curtain of water . . .
like too much Persephone and not enough underworld . . .
wearing nothing but an arts degree . . .
and the soft blowtorch of their eyes . . .

You can feel their judgments come down upon you
like too-heavy butterflies . . .
but there's nothing you can do about it!
and worst of all
they don't even want anything . . .
they're just standing there . . .
re-mentioning Deleuze and Guattari
in loneliness and natural lighting

The ex-girlfriends are back
like the liquidation sale of an imported rug megastore
that's been liquidating for centuries . . .
getting rich off all that... tasselled goodbye money
as they grind your face yet again into
the hand-knotted . . .
semi-Persian wool blend . . . of their hearts
begging once more for closure

The ex-girlfriends are back
with their sanity pangs
and various life fatigues . . .
like a stuffed-crocodile exhibit
still begging for death relevance
in the glass case of your heart
But you are the museum director now!
Walking talent on a stiff gold leash
& there's nothing anyone can do about it!

## PLANET OF THE APES

If there is a designated point at which return
becomes of no return, so far is how far

I am always beyond it.
We sit in the rain of your hangover

and I tell you the story about my dead aunt
who spent her sixteenth year digging a giant hole

in the field behind her house and never said why.
Anna, I love you.

I love you in the jittering shade of a historic windmill.
I love you standing in the water wearing the river

like an invisible pair of shoes. I love you here
at the beginning of your only life and almost gone

getting high on your porch, light drifting between us
like ghost sequins.

I've always never felt this way about anyone
but the way in which I've never felt about you

is a way of never feeling so new it's somehow old
like a cave painting of a fax machine

or falling asleep in the attic of a spaceship.
You make me want to think of you in a sentence with me in it.

You make me want to find a collapsed mineshaft
I can call your name in while searching for you.

You make me want to tell you what you make me want
but what can I even say to you—riding a desk chair

through the afternoon like the patron saint
of remaindered office furniture.

I don't know what it means
to walk each night into a field alone

and dig until you are standing in a hole so deep
you cannot be seen above ground.

I don't know what it means to fall asleep on your porch
and wake with the illustrated guide to Planet of the Apes open in my hands.

I don't know what it means to wake each morning and love you
and say nothing, as if nothing

were honesty's default, or maybe just a way
for me to avoid the stupid things I need to tell you like

looking at you is like looking at a beautiful person far away
through a telescope that makes you seem the size you almost are

which is something I mean but don't understand
like the new hieroglyphics of songbirds

or how the world in which I'm saying this to you
is already receding

that looking at you is like looking
backwards out the window of a slow-moving helicopter

into the nineteenth-century cornfield of your face
which my historical inaccuracy

has suddenly emptied of birds.
You make my life feel the size of itself.

You make my life a burning craft
on some distant and unintended hillside.

Anna you are the pale green arm
of the Statue of Liberty

reaching up through miles of sand

# BISEXUALITY

*There's such a thing as too much sexual freedom . . .*
Heidegger wrote that and he was bisexual too
always naked on a black leash, scrubbing the telephone
You think, my heart is a shanty town . . . with fur curtains blowing

It's like turning your back on God........... but in a risqué halter neck
Like a rocking horse at auction you go to the highest bidder
You want to come home, but your home was destroyed in the war. . . .
And carefully refurbished, with an elegant leopard trim

The men are bad, and the girls...................... are worse bad
Each day you wake up and have to be the wife again
To be a woman to a woman, is a female double-jointedness
Your heart a black salt lick, in an elk-laden pasture

To be bisexual is to be out of office, even to yourself
Like a rare sexual Narnia and no spring in sight
They won't let you out of the closet to get back in again
Deep in the winter coats, a little snow starts falling . . .

Everyone assumes you want to fuck them......... and they're right
but you're also bad girl, with a kinky . . . goodbye fetish
Always bursting into tears in the hotel lobby!
Gliding off in a taxi, with a briefcase full of military secrets

It's hard to know what bisexuality means
It just....... comes over you, like an urban sandstorm
When a fish crawls up onto land?—that's bisexuality
It's an ancient sexual amphibiousness

It's like climbing out of a burning building into too much water
Or climbing out of a burning building.......
into a second identical burning building
Why does everything have to be so on fire? you ask yourself
But when you look down, your fretwork is smoking

Not the well of loneliness, more like a water feature
But a tasteful one, with a hidden power supply
You look out over the hills and the rows of red houses
And worst of all, you don't even like softball!!!

## WASTE MY LIFE

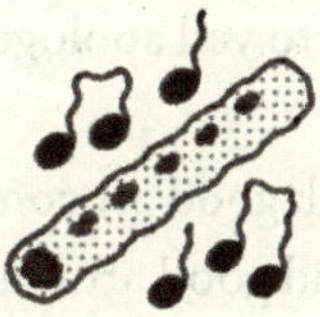

sleep, boredom, gossip, cruelty
imaginary feuds and small resentments
various, complex plans that amount to nothing
at some point, you have to admit
art is a distraction from the boredom of life

I work all day in a bookshop
each night I come home
and the rain is falling
covering the world in black diamonds
some days I feel so deep inside my life I don't think I'll ever get out

I've never read the Russians but I have read most of the Babysitters Club
I can't remember the meaning of poetry
other than it's a broken telephone
with which to call the dead
and tell them a joke

life is great
it's like being given a rare and historically significant flute
and using it to beat a harmless old man to death

I used to think the more something hurt, the more meaningful it was
but I never learned anything useful from pain
I just drank a bottle of wine and tried to fall asleep

when you're unhappy you can't think
pain is just boredom with the stars turned up

there's not much I like in this world
I'm always walking away too early in a conversation
and having to yell apologetically back over my shoulder

I don't think good art comes from happiness either
but who said good art was the point

## WATCHING SIX SEASONS OF THE NANNY WHILE MY RELATIONSHIP SLOWLY FELL APART

Maxwell chased Fran up and down the staircase
I lay in bed, listening to the distant sound of trains
Pulling their shit-for-brains cargo through the dark
There are some months when all art feels worthless
And life feels thin, and weak and full of spite
Often I think about the man who walked into the National Gallery
And punched a hole straight into a ten million-dollar Monet painting
Of a sailboat, drifting down a river of autumn leaves
And got sent to prison for five years

There's nothing in this world more boring than heartbreak
It's like a tax audit of the soul
And what once seemed rare and poignant
And full of emotional promise
Just makes me want to dose myself to the brim with horse tranquilizers
And take a long vacation to skeleton town

The present has overflowed and turned the whole past bad
Ancient Greece, art nouveau, the entire Italian renaissance
All ruined
Monet too, with his surfeit of waterlilies
Wilting in the heat like a loose-leaf salad
I sit like Nostradamus
In my kingdom of disappointment
Burning down the cities of the future
Going through my google calendar
listing all the bad things to come

# WILD GEESE BY MARY OLIVER BY HERA LINDSAY BIRD

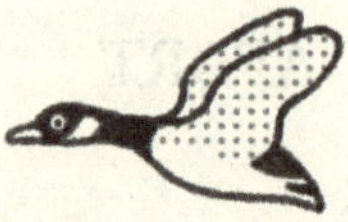

*You do not have to be good*
is everything you deserve for taking
relationship advice from a flock of migratory birds.
Even in poetry I forgive you nothing
not even your new empire of grief.
You take off your dress and stand in the river
your body a ghost on loan
from someone else's past.
*Tell me about your despair, yours, and I will tell you mine.*
Meanwhile in a hospital gown
Meanwhile in a long-dead language
Meanwhile every morning, the stars in tatters on the snow
Meanwhile the library of Alexandria burning in alphabetical order
Meanwhile an asterisk blowing across the screen like tumbleweed
Meanwhile every day for the rest of our lives
I return here to ask you how to forgive someone
who was never mine to forgive.

*You do not have to be good*
Being good isn't even the point anymore.
I just don't think it's real
to think of geese and feel so beautiful about yourself
and so far away.
Yesterday my girlfriend and I borrowed a car
and drove down through the valley
where my mother almost starved herself to death twenty years ago
a huge silver wind blowing in from the sea.
What do I care if there's no justice in this world?
Life is hard

and pain is hard
and it's hard for me to write plainly
about the night my girlfriend told me she still loved you and call it art.
It did not feel like art.
It did not feel like *a hundred miles through the desert repenting.*
It did not feel like a broken wheel backwards into the sea
But it hurt me.
It still hurts me
Even now
The shadow of new leaves trembling the carpet.

Oh Mary
How will we survive ourselves
And will this life ever answer?
I don't know
Panic and awe are the same to me.
I love life
and I hate death
so when you try to describe to me
what it feels like to want to die
I can only look at you
like you are a slow-burning planet
and I am pouring water through a telescope.

*You do not have to be good.*
You do not have to be anything.
This is not an anthem for the world.
This life is a hard life and
it crushes people
But it's also weird and full of heat
Crocodiles asleep in their red tent of hunger.
Puzzle pieces blown up the street
On the road outside the house
We sold all our things and moved south for.

It was winter and we were so in love
Sitting on the floor of her grandmother's house
watching the news roll in
about the woman who had been chained
for seven years in someone's basement
And just got free.
The next morning we packed all our things and headed south.
As if it were that easy.
As if there were anywhere to arrive
We could ever return from.

# WINTER

# JEALOUSY

Anytime someone I love mentions someone they used to date
in a semi-nostalgic or non-cynical way
I immediately want to drive my car
head-first into a swamp full of battery acid
ruining Christmas for everyone!!!!!
it's so unreasonable
to be afraid of so many sad and distant women
who have escaped into the future
only occasionally looking back through their naturally thick eyelashes

When I think about the possibility
the person I'm with has ever been romantically interested
in another person ever
I felt a great self-antagonism
for being the kind of woman who came afterwards
like a bad sequel with a higher budget
O I feel sorry for the people I love and where I'm taking them
because I don't think I'm good enough
I think it's okay to admit the people you love are better than you
I wouldn't date anyone who wasn't
imagine dating someone worse than yourself on purpose
that's the kind of fucked up thing only everyone I've ever loved would do

## I WILL ALREADY REMEMBER YOU FOR THE REST OF MY LIFE

Standing on your balcony in winter I think:
I will already remember you for the rest of my life
It's too late now, I know who you are
and what you look like
and must henceforth venture through life recalling you many times
as you continue to make things difficult
by reminding yourself to me more and more
by taking me to various locations and describing to me your . . . aspirations
some ancient moon smouldering above us

I will always think of you and how it was between us
and the things you did and said

I will think about your personality and your interests
and the specific colour of your hair and eyes
Even if we have a terrific breakup and stop calling each other
I'll still remember you
I won't be able to help it! You're there in my memory
like the concept of opera. Or the Simpsons theme song.
Like a field of blossoms in an air freshener commercial
sarcastic with light
I will think of your temperament and your enthusiasms
and how you looked at me
I will think of all the things you told me about your life

# BRUCE WILLIS YOU ARE THE GHOST

It's not that your wife doesn't love you. It's because you died and now you're a ghost and she can't hear you talking to her. That time you saw her taking off her wedding ring? It's because you're her dead husband and she can't continue to mourn your absence with heterosexual jewellery indefinitely. Stop haunting her already Bruce Willis! Bruce Willis, it's hard to be a ghost and not know you are a ghost. Haven't you noticed the only person you've talked to in a year is a supernaturally gifted child? Don't you think it's weird your wife just cries alone in the living room every night, re-watching your wedding tape and never looking or speaking to you? Don't you remember being fatally shot in the stomach at the beginning of the movie? Walk towards the light, Bruce Willis. Walk towards the light.

# THE PROBLEM WITH BEING A WOMAN

I don't know what my problem is, but it's bigger than you
it's bigger than me even
this problem—whatever it is
has made me very drunk on a Wednesday night

I feel a great loneliness which is to be the person who is always looking
I have looked at the world my whole life
out from behind my eyes
I have looked at other people and wondered what they're thinking

when I'm in love I can only think about one thing which is being in love
to me what freedom is
is to be able to think of whatever you want all the time
a cat who is also a dentist
a wheelbarrow full of silver snakes

I think if there was someone who loved me as much as I loved them
I would have to frown at them in disapproval
I look into the faces of the men I love when they're looking away
there is a great freedom there, like a president communing with an evil
    mountain
a black and purple mountain with crazy trees and lightning coming off it

I am drunk and crazy but I know what I am talking about
to be a woman is to be half-alive
to love someone in a muscle shirt
while they polish their car in hunky ignorance

maybe it's just the way the world is
that loving someone is always going to involve a deep kind of loneliness

and the closer you get to understanding someone
the more you understand how fundamentally un-understandable other
    people are

there is a great loneliness to being in love
there is a great loneliness to standing outside at night
and looking at a hillside of sloping, dark-green trees

I think there are other kinds of loneliness, which are more advanced
like the kind of loneliness serious men have
where they look god in the eye and decide to die

I would never die
or, at least, it wouldn't be for a good reason
if i died it would only be to make someone else mad
that's the problem with being a woman

## MONICA

Monica
Monica
Monica
Monica Geller from popular sitcom F.R.I.E.N.D.S
Is one of the worst characters in the history of television
She makes me want to wash my eyes with hand sanitiser
She makes me want to stand in an abandoned Ukrainian parking lot
And scream her name at a bunch of dead crows
Nobody liked her, except for Chandler
He married her, and that brings me to my second point
What kind of a name for a show was F.R.I.E.N.D.S
When two of them were related
And the rest of them just fucked for ten seasons?
Maybe their fucking was secondary to their friendship
Or they all had enough emotional equilibrium
To be able to maintain a constant state of mutual respect
Despite the fucking
Or conspicuous nonfucking
That was occurring in their lives
But I have to say
It just doesn't seem emotionally realistic
Especially considering that
They were not the most self-aware people
And to be able to maintain a friendship
Through the various complications of heterosexual monogamy
Is enormously difficult
Especially when you take into consideration
What cunts they all were

I fell in love with a friend once

And we liked to congratulate each other on what good friends we were
And how it was great we could be such good friends, and still fuck
Until we stopped fucking
And then we weren't such good friends anymore

I had a dream the other night
About this friend, and how we were walking
Through sunlight, many years ago
Dragged up from the vaults, like old military propaganda
You know the kind; young women leaving a factory
Arm in arm, while their fiancées
Are being handsomely shot to death in Prague
And even though this friend doesn't love me anymore
And I don't love them
At least, not in a romantic sense
The memory of what it had been like not to want
To strap a concrete block to my head
And drown myself in a public fountain rather than spend another day
With them not talking to me
Came back, and I remembered the world
For a moment, as it had been
When we had just met, and love seemed possible
And neither of us resented the other one
And it made me sad
Not just because things ended badly
But more broadly
Because my sadness had less to do with the emotional specifics of that situation
And more to do with the transitory nature of romantic love
Which is becoming relevant to me once again
Because I just met someone new
And this dream reminded me
That, although I believe there are ways that love can endure
It's just that statistically, or

Based on personal experience,
It's unlikely that things are going to go well for long
There is such a narrow window
For happiness in this life
And if the past is anything to go by
Everything is about to go slowly but inevitably wrong
In a non-confrontational but ultimately disappointing way

Monica
Monica
Monica
Monica Geller from popular sitcom F.R.I.E.N.D.S
Was the favourite character of the Uber driver
Who drove me home the other day
And is the main reason for this poem
Because I remember thinking *Monica???*
Maybe he doesn't remember who she is
Because when I asked him specifically
Which character he liked best off F.R.I.E.N.D.S
He said *the woman*
And when I listed their names for him
Phoebe, Rachel, and Monica
He said *Monica?*
But he said it with a kind of question mark at the end
Which led me to believe
He didn't know who he was talking about
And had got her confused with one of the other
Less objectively terrible characters

I think the driver meant to say Phoebe
Because Phoebe is everyone's favourite
She once stabbed a police officer
She once gave birth to her brother's triplets
She doesn't give a shit what anyone thinks about her

Monica gives a shit what everyone thinks about her
Monica's parents didn't treat her very well
And that's probably where a lot of her underlying insecurities come from
That have since manifested themselves in controlling and manipulative behaviour
It's not that I think Monica is unredeemable
I can recognise that her personality has been shaped
By a desire to succeed
And that even when she did succeed, it was never enough
Particularly for her mother, who made her feel like her dreams were stupid
And a waste of time
And that kind of constant belittlement can do really fucked up things to a person
So maybe getting upset when people don't use coasters
Is an understandable or at least comparatively sane response
To the psychic baggage
Of your parents never having believed in you

Often I look at the world
And I am dumbfounded anyone can function at all
Given the kinds of violence that
So many people have inherited from the past
But that's still no excuse to throw
A dinner plate at your friends during a quiet game of Pictionary
And even if that was an isolated incident
And she was able to move on from it
It still doesn't make me want to watch her on TV
I am falling in love and I don't know what to do about it
Throw me in a haunted wheelbarrow and set me on fire
And don't even get me started on Ross

## KEATS IS DEAD SO FUCK ME FROM BEHIND

Keats is dead, so fuck me from behind
Slowly and with carnal purpose
Some black midwinter afternoon
While all the children are walking home from school
Peel my stockings down with your teeth
Coleridge is dead, and Auden too
Of laughing in an overcoat
Shelley died at sea and his heart wouldn't burn
And Wordsworth......
They never found his body
His widow mad with grief, hammering nails into an empty meadow
Byron, Whitman, our dog crushed by a garage door
Finger me slowly
In the snowscape of your childhood
Our dead floating just below the earth's surface
Bend me over like a substitute teacher
& pump me full of shivering arrows
O emotional vulnerability
Bosnian folk-song, birds in the chimney
Tell me what you love when you think I'm not listening
Wallace Stevens's mother is calling him
But he's not coming, he died sixty years ago
And nobody cared at his funeral
Life is real
And the days burn off like leopard print
Nobody, not even the dead can tell me what to do
Eat my pussy from behind
Bill Manhire's not getting any younger

# HAVING SEX IN A FIELD IN 2013

Is the title of this poem, but it's also a true story about being in love
I am in love with you
While one bird feeds another bird right next to me
they throw their shadows into my life
like black sugar
I love to feel this bad because it reminds me of being human
I love this life too
Every day something new happens and I think
so this is the way things are now
I thought that as a stranger put his tongue between my legs
in the first hour of the New Year
and again as I woke
to a field of slow-blowing trees
and right now telling you
Friends, I love everything new
even the first days of heartbreak
when everything beautiful is set alight
the glass fur of the cactus
birds on fire with wonder
I have done many things in my life
I have talked to many people
Some of these people have called me drunk at one in the morning
These people are my best friends
They are like miles of snow to me
When I listen to my voicemail
I can hear one of them saying
Did she just hang up on us

# HAVING ALREADY WALKED OUT ON EVERYONE I EVER SAID I LOVED

I pause for a moment at your door
And consult my fate
This life is more stupid than I could have hoped for
Every day a search party gets lost in the snow
With no one to dig them out again
I have tried for too long to act in ways that seem reasonable
Yet somehow, this makes me double-unreasonable
Like flicking someone's bra strap at a coroner's inquest
The official theme of this poem is
The official theme of all my poems which is
You get in love and then you die!
Oh write it in rhinestones on the lid of my coffin
Some people are too hard to be lived without

Once upon a time I used to feel like............huh
But then I started to feel a little more like..................................uhuh

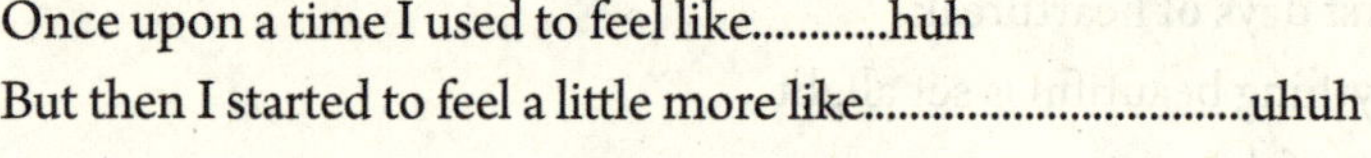

Once upon a time I used to feel like.................??
But then I started to feel a little more like................................????????

Having already walked out on everyone I ever said I loved
Things do not bode well for you
But things do also not bode well for me
Every year life gets less and less acceptable
And I feel uncertain of how to proceed in an appropriate fashion
To anticipate heartache is a grim satisfaction
Like tripping down a staircase in a peach negligee
Or an ancient forest with a new corsage of flames
It pleases me to subject myself to such whimsical hurt feelings

But under my main feelings I have other worse feelings
Like an auxiliary moat in which black swans are circling
If I ever die young I'm going to do it in style
. . . like a Great Gatsby-themed suicide attempt!

Having already walked out on everyone I ever said I loved
I have so little left to say to you
I pause for a moment at your door
My eyes pouring out across the darkness

Oh let us not be little bitches to one another
Life is hard enough as it is
Life is hard enough and fast enough
And there's nothing in this world worth doing
But shaking our heads in awe

A little wind shifts the branches
A bird flies out of the radio and off into silence

I can hardly believe this
I can hardly believe this life
Every time I knock you let me in

# SPRING

# I KNEW I LOVED YOU WHEN YOU SHOWED ME YOUR MINECRAFT WORLD

It wasn't the upside-down crosses in your mansion
or even the lone, giant cigarette burning in the sky.
You walked me around and I watched the back of your head
suddenly overcome by the feeling of knowing
I was beyond what could be recovered from
the dark pixels of the forest vibrating in a virtual wind
distant panpipe music blowing through your speakers
It's not that I didn't love you before
it is just—there are some things which cannot be said
and some feelings which, if articulated too early
and forced towards the surface, go blind
& it's better to hold them off or wait them out
& never say their name aloud until the pressure of what is unspoken
becomes impossible to hold back
and articulates itself within the body
like mice, running wild through a field of burning grass.
The train disappears underground and comes back up again
The cigarette distributes its vague cancers into the sky
twilight's firing shadows like a t-shirt gun
And spring is on the wind like wifi
When I was miserable you came and showed me card tricks
When the moon was full we pissed into the bushes like animals
I watch you sleep, like a security guard looking at a famous painting
through a searchlight
walk me to the graveyard on the edge of your map
nothing must hurt you, not even me

# MIRROR TRAPS

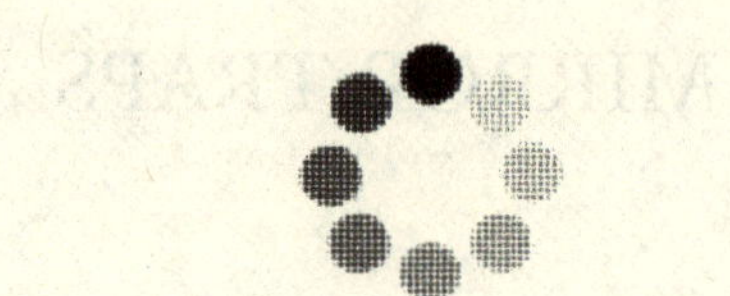

I want to lie naked &

face down

in the beige epicentre
of my despair

/

against the fringed tessellations
of an inner-city graveyard

tombstones wilting in the heat

like black candles

I want to lie alone &
    trembling
in my hot     neural vacancy

like a jet shadow

across a distant field of corn

emitting
many slow     blinks of the heart

& never have a job

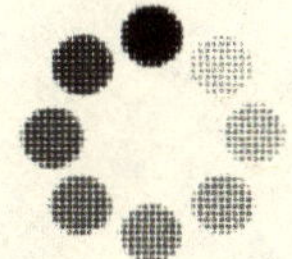

I want to lie each night
in the overlapping heat

of your absence

&

shuck my heart

into fresh transparencies

of repentant love

black pheromones pour out of your eyeholes

mirrors curl        in the sunlight

you smile at me &
cool beads float through my heart

like the inner pellets
of a frozen baby rattle

&

the overall ache
of never having touched you

wedged
like a double-sided battle-axe
in the cleft of an antique rocking chair

still rocking

with its slow elliptical

murder force

the soft black
drumroll of your gaze
breaks over me
like a molten wave of snow
& my heart

blinks

& flares

like the yellow gills of a taxicab

when you look at me
with your soft austerity

like baby epaulettes

It's bad poetry to have a body
    & want to touch you with it

even worse............. to be allowed to
            as you stare at me

                    across the silence

of your rare anti-camouflague

& tell me what it is you have wanted

It's bad poetry to have a body
and a bad life too

to get everything you wanted
but still walk away
for no other reason

but........... the unspecified wrongness of your blood

& all you can do
is lie face down on the carpet

& wait for the heart to finish buffering

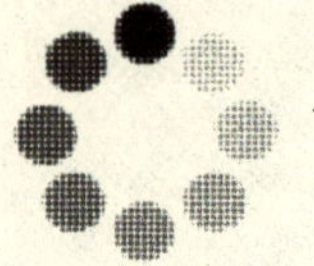

it's love that plummets you
        back down the elevator shaft

& it's love you go missing to

buying candles from an inner-city megastore

there is something wrong with you

there is something wrong with you that is also wrong with me

I want to lie very still

in a discount facial peel

cucumber slices
floating on my eyelids

like a double-salad monocle

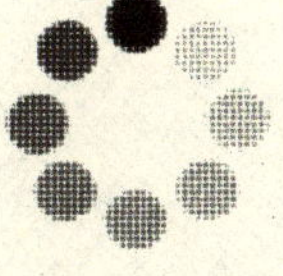

I want to stare    out the window

in a deep    optic hunger

until everything burns

with the mohair of loneliness

& never be touched

I want to lie awake each night

& be struck by
oscillating waves of

regret

the heart like a cold sleigh drawn
again & again

through the dark avenues of spring

always towards your silence

## SALAD DAYS

Eve was the first woman
naked as a moon in daylight
She wore a leaf on her crotch
like a healthful garnish

Beautiful Eve
She ruined things for the rest of us
& God never forgave her for it.

Stupid God
Scooping up handfuls of raw birds
And eating them like popcorn

He's like Kevin Sorbo
He's got wet mice for brains
He didn't know a good thing when he saw it.

# LOVE COMES BACK

Like your father,
twenty years later with the packet of cigarettes he went out for
Like Monday but this is the nineteenth century
& you're a monied aristocrat with no conception of the working week
Like a haunted board game
pried from the rubble of an archaeological dig site
You roll the dice & bats come flooding out your heart
like molten grappling hooks
your resolve weakening . . .
like the cord of an antique disco ball . . .
Love like the recurring decimal of some huge, indivisible number
or a well-thrown boomerang
coming to rest in the soft curve of your hand
Love comes back . . .
like a murderer returning to the scene of the crime . . .
or not returning . . .
yet still the crime remains . . .
like love . . .
observed or unobserved . . .
written in blood on the walls of some ancient civilisation
in an idiom so old
we have no contemporary vernacular equivalent

Love like Windows 95
The greatest, most user-friendly Windows of them all
Those four little panes of light
Like the stained glass of an ancient church
vibrating in the sunlit rubble
of the twentieth century
Your face comes floating up in my crystal ball . . .

The lights come on at the bottom of the ocean
& here we are alone again . . .

Late November
we ride the black escalator of the mountain
& emerge into the altitude of our last year
The rabbit in the grass gives us something wild to aim for
It twists into spring like a living bell

I have to be here always telling you that
no matter how far I travel beyond you
love will stay tethered
like an evil kite I want to always reel back in
As if we could just turn and wade back
through the ghost of some ancient season
or wake each morning in the heat of a vanished life

Love comes back
from where it's never gone . . . It was here the whole time
like a genetic anomaly waiting to reveal itself
Like spring at the museum, after centuries of silence
the bronze wings of gladiator helmets trembling in their sockets . . .
Grecian urns sprouting new leaves . . .
Love like a hand from the grave
trembling up into the sunlight of the credit sequence
the names of the dead
pouring down the screen
like cool spring rain

## NEW THINGS

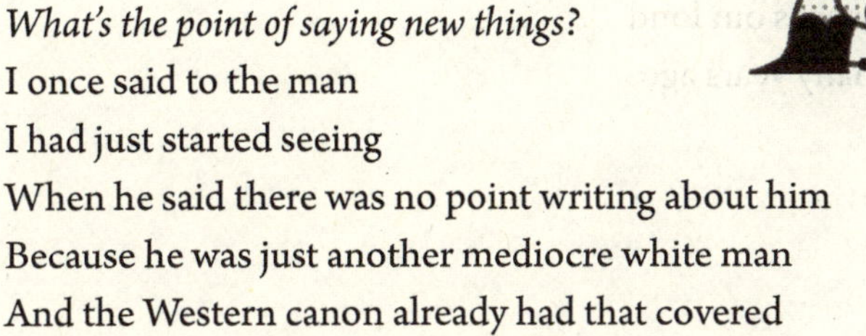

*What's the point of saying new things?*
I once said to the man
I had just started seeing
When he said there was no point writing about him
Because he was just another mediocre white man
And the Western canon already had that covered

What is there to say about the world that hasn't already been?
More to the point,
Who gives a shit?
Three-thousand-years of standing at the lakeside
Mourning the fall of the Byzantine Empire
I'm as bored of it as anyone
and Shakespeare too
We should all move to the country and fuck each other's brains out

Still, there are better things to be than original
So maybe I can say jazz apothecary
Or ham pantyliner
But it gives me no pleasure
To mean so little
And get so far away with it

What is there to say about love that hasn't already been
Three-thousand-years of grass and wind
We lay on the banks of the field behind your house
Oh there is nothing to do in this life

The world describes itself again
Black curtains on the windows, pinned up with needles

All across the field, small lights falling
Like snow on a virgin rollercoaster
And trees, I am still crazy
I can barely look at you
I can barely say the words out loud
I could be dead so many years ago

## PAIN IMPERATIVES

*After Chelsey Minnis*

You have to slap yourself in the face with a mohair glove
You have to challenge yourself to a mini-duel
You have to rub your hands on your thighs and think about pain
A little pain comes on, and you get tiresome again

The past is a bad invention that keeps on happening
And it hurts to think about, like an unpaid bill
It's the wind dragging the desert backwards at night
& it burns you, like a little silver whip

You have to think like this all day in a cucumber facemask
You have to lie very still and wish you were dead
You have to think *love has radicalised me* & walk around like Helen of Troy
You have to walk around until the ships burn off

It's so sad to be in love and not enough of it
It's so sad to be in love and not be still
It's so sad to be with someone so sad
It's so sad to want to

It’s a bad crime to say poetry in poetry
It’s a bad, adorable crime
Like robbing a bank with a mini-hairdryer
I should never do it—and nor should anyone
But it’s boring to be so tasteful
It’s like never masturbating to Lucy Liu

Poetry should be democratic—that's the modern view
It's like a murder on a train where everyone did it!
This is a shared misery, like crying someone else to sleep
It's like the sugared hole at the top of the mountain where the flag goes in

You have to look people in the eye, and say 'uh oh'
You have to drag your heart across the room like a heavy chair
You have to tell yourself what you need and do the opposite
You have to be staggered by the cruelty of it

You have to stay up each night as a love punishment
You have to handcuff yourself to the past and swallow the key
You have to make a career out of your pain
You have to pinch yourself and think ow like you mean it

This is breathing through a megaphone
Or begging for mercy in a Russian phrasebook
I write this poem like an obituary in Comic Sans
I write it like suicide hotline hold music

This is dull propaganda—like stock footage of the heart
This is opening your trenchcoat to reveal another trenchcoat
This is a well-choreographed melodrama—with a complimentary
    fainting chair
It gets you smoking in a gold kimono

This is a birdbath overflowing with Mountain Dew
It's like doing a line of sherbet off a toilet seat
This is a prim vulgarity, like a well-starched nipple tassel
This is putting on mascara to cry yourself to sleep

This is a Pyrrhic victory, like falling in love
It's having so little to say, you hire a skywriter to stay home
This is storming out in the middle of a bar fight, your bonnet strands
streaming
You cry and cry, impressing no one

You think you know the world and then it changes
Time caves in and obliterates the heart
it's like using a jackhammer to bust open a music box
the box cracks, and minor notes come drifting out

Poetry is a fake nostalgia
It rears up behind you on its antique leg brace
This is a higher truth, like a haunted polygraph
It's a church billboard blowing down the interstate

Who was it that said *the life we enter is not the one we leave*?*
It's an arcane law, like falling in love
It's like a game of musical chairs, but they keep adding more chairs
You get up to leave, but the gramophone goes on and on

* Mary Ruefle

This is: stop hitting yourself!
It's pushing a pork roast in a vintage pram
This is an empty cuckoo clock, fast approaching midnight
This is a ransom note with no demands

# PYRAMID SCHEME

*for RWT*

the other day I was thinking about the term Pyramid Scheme
and why they called it Pyramid Scheme and not triangle scheme
I asked you what you thought
you thought it added a certain gravitas and linked the idea of economic prosperity
with some of history's greatest archaeological achievements
unconsciously suggesting a silent wealth of gold and heat

a triangle is two-dimensional, and therefore
a less striking mental image than the idea of a third dimension of financial fraud which is how many
dimensions of financial fraud the term pyramid scheme suggests
but I had to pause for a second at the financial fraud part
because it occurred to me I didn't know what pyramid schemes really were

I knew they had something to do with people getting money from nothing like
the person at the top of the pyramid scheme
acquires a number of investors and takes their money
and then pays the first lot of investors with the money from another bunch of investors
and so on and so forth
all the way to the bottom of the triangle
or pyramid face
which is the kind of stupid thing that happens
if you keep your money in a pyramid and not a bank account
although if you ask me banks are the real pyramid schemes after all
or was love the real pyramid scheme? I can't remember

maybe its better to keep your money in a pyramid than a bank
and I should shop around and compare the interest rates on different

pyramids
maybe I should open up a savings pyramid
with a whole bunch of trapdoors and malarias
to keep the financial anthropologists
I mean bankers out
my emeralds cooling under the ground like beautiful women's eyes

I think this was supposed to be a metaphor for something
but I can't remember where I was going with it
and now it's been swept away by the winds of
whatever
but knowing me, it was probably love
That great dark blue sex hope that keeps coming true
That cartoon black castle with a single bird flying over it

I don't know where this poem ends
how far below the sand
but it's still early evening
and you and I are a little drunk

you answer the phone
you pour me a drink
i know you hate the domestic in poetry but you should have thought of
 that before you asked me to move in with you

i used to think arguments were the same as honesty
i used to think screaming was the same as passion
i used to think pain was meaningful
i no longer think pain is meaningful
i never learned anything good from being unhappy
i never learned anything good from being happy either
the way i feel about you has nothing to do with learning
it has nothing to do with anything
but i feel it down in the corners of my sarcophagus

i feel it in my sleep
even when i am not thinking about you
you are still pouring through my blood, like fire
through an abandoned hospital ward
these coins are getting heavy on my eyes
it has been a great honour and privilege to love you
it is a great honour and privilege to eat cold pizza on your steps at dawn
love is so stupid: it's like punching the sun
and having a million gold coins rain down on you
which you don't even have to pay tax on
because sun money is free money
and I'm pretty sure there are no laws about that
but I would pay tax
because I believe hospitals and education
and the arts should be publicly funded
even this poem
when I look at you
my eyes are two identical neighbourhood houses on fire
when I look at you
my eyes bulge out of my skull like a dog in a cartoon
when I am with you
an enormous silence descends upon me
and i feel like i am sinking into the deepest part of my life
we walk down the street, with the grass blowing back and forth
i have never been so happy

**HERA LINDSAY BIRD** is a poet from New Zealand. She is the author of chapbook *Pamper Me to Hell & Back* (The Poetry Business, 2018) and a self-titled debut collection, which became a best-seller in New Zealand and a *Sunday Times* Book of the Year.